Where Did the **Dinosaurs** Go?

C. Vance Cast
Illustrated by Sue Wilkinson

Hi, I'm Clever Calvin, and this is my friend Denise. She is a *paleontologist.* Paleontologists are scientists who study the remains of plants and animals that have been dead for millions of years.

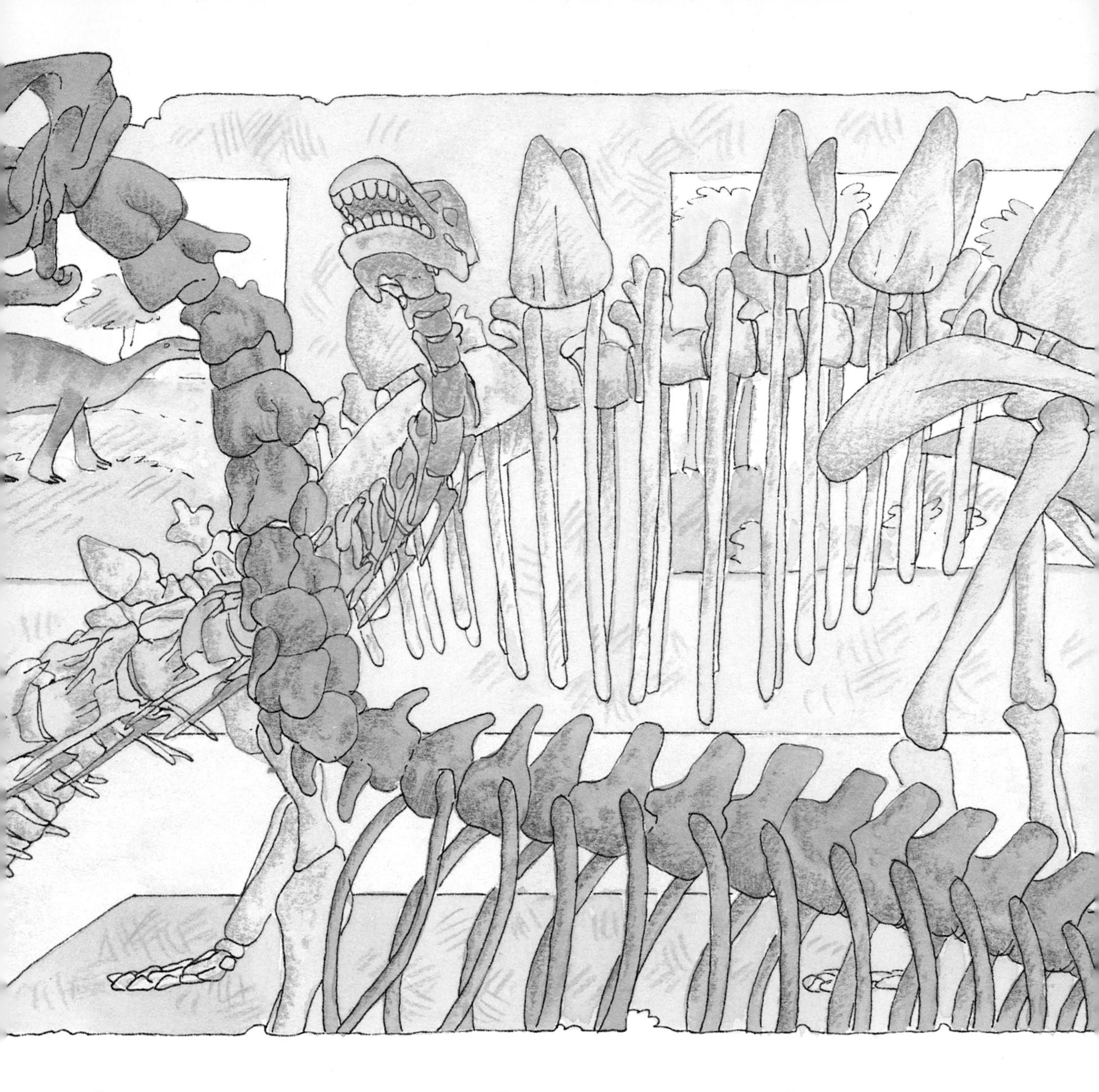

These remains, preserved in stone, are called *fossils.* Today, Denise has been showing me dinosaur fossils here at the Museum of Natural Science.

This dinosaur certainly is enormous! In fact, the biggest animals that ever lived on land were dinosaurs. For millions of years they ruled the Earth.

But now they are all gone. What happened to them? Are they hiding somewhere? Or have they disappeared forever?

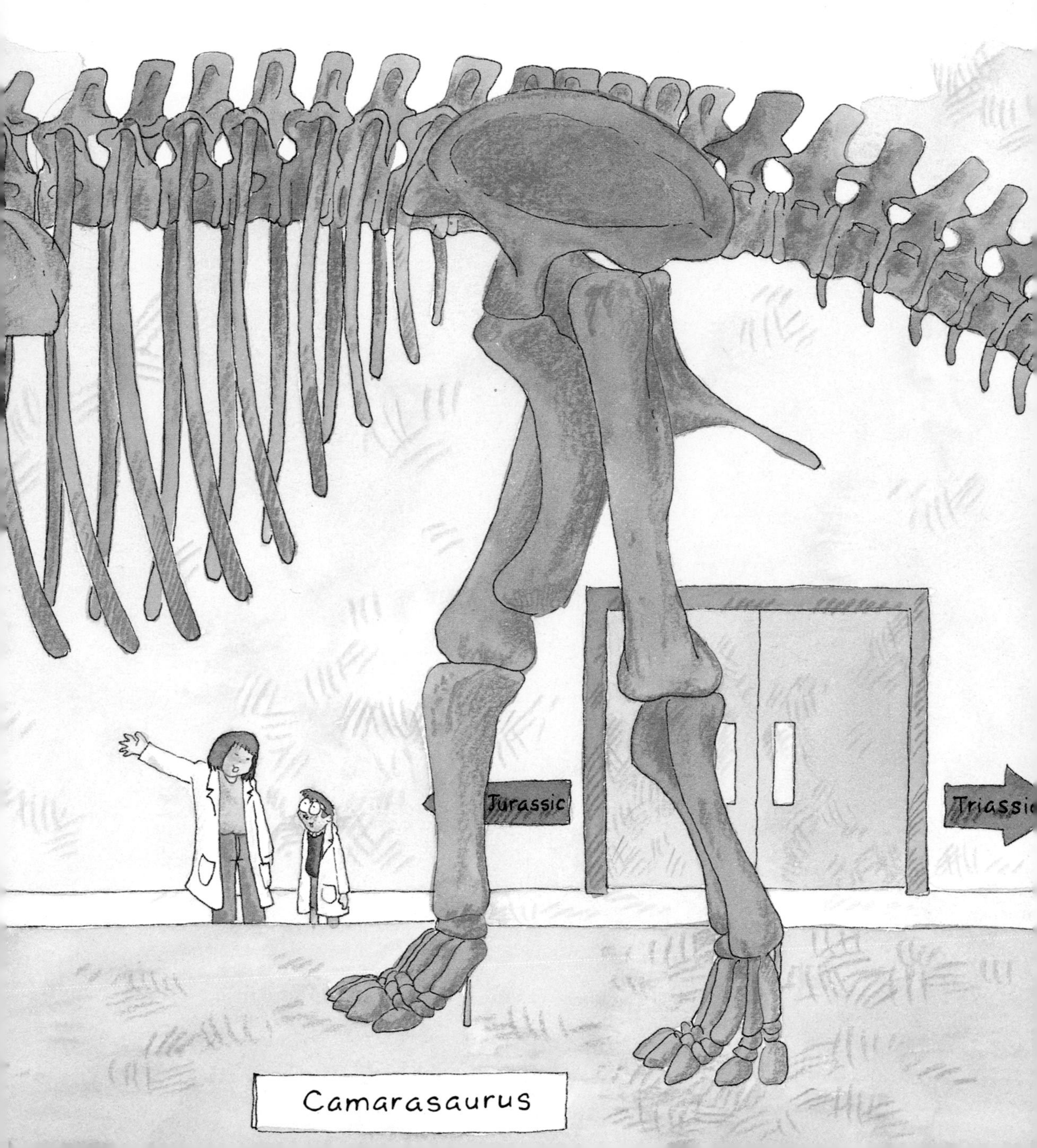

These are all great questions to try to answer, but first let's learn a little bit about dinosaurs and the world they lived in.

The word dinosaur comes from two Greek words that mean "terrible lizard." Yes, some dinosaurs were gigantic and terrifying. But, they were not really lizards—although they do look something like them.

Dinosaurs were *reptiles,* a grouping that includes lizards, snakes, turtles, alligators, and crocodiles. Like lizards, dinosaurs had scaly skin and laid eggs. But dinosaurs' legs were long and grew under their bodies.

Lizards' legs are short and grow out to their sides. Because of this difference, dinosaurs could walk and run much better than lizards.

Dinosaurs lived on Earth during the *Mesozoic era*—a very long period that lasted from about 250 million until about 65 million years ago. During this time, giant reptiles lived in the sea....

Other reptiles soared through the air—
some on leathery 15-foot (4.6-meter)
wings....

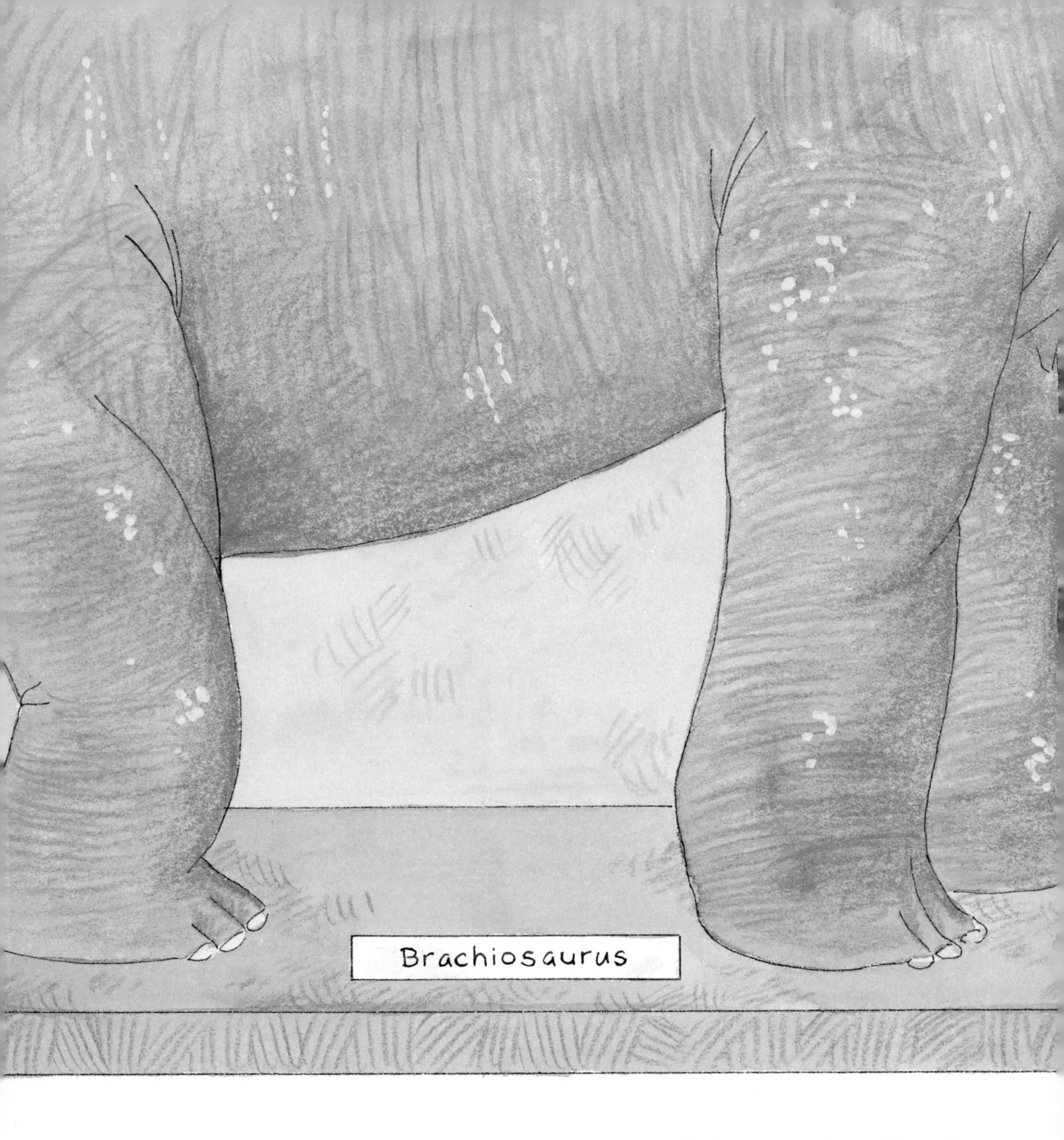

And on the ground walked many different kinds of dinosaurs. Some were big enough to shake the earth—like this 39-foot (12-meter) tall *Brachiosaurus.*

And some were very small like the *Compsognathus*. This dinosaur was about the same size as a chicken.

We learn what we know about dinosaurs by studying fossils of their bones. By examining a single leg bone, Denise can estimate the size of the dinosaur.

By looking at the head, or even just a tooth or a claw, she can tell us what kind of food it ate.

Meat eaters, called *carnivores,* had big powerful heads with rows of long teeth that curved back so they could rip and chew their prey. This *Tyrannosaurus rex* also had sharp claws on its front feet for grabbing and holding its prey.

Plant eaters, called *herbivores,* often had long necks so they could reach the leaves of tall trees.

Diplodocus had finger-like front teeth for raking leaves into its mouth. Because it had no back teeth for chewing, it had to swallow its food whole.

Hadrosaurus had a duckbill-like snout and hundreds of sharp diamond-shaped teeth for grinding and shredding plants.

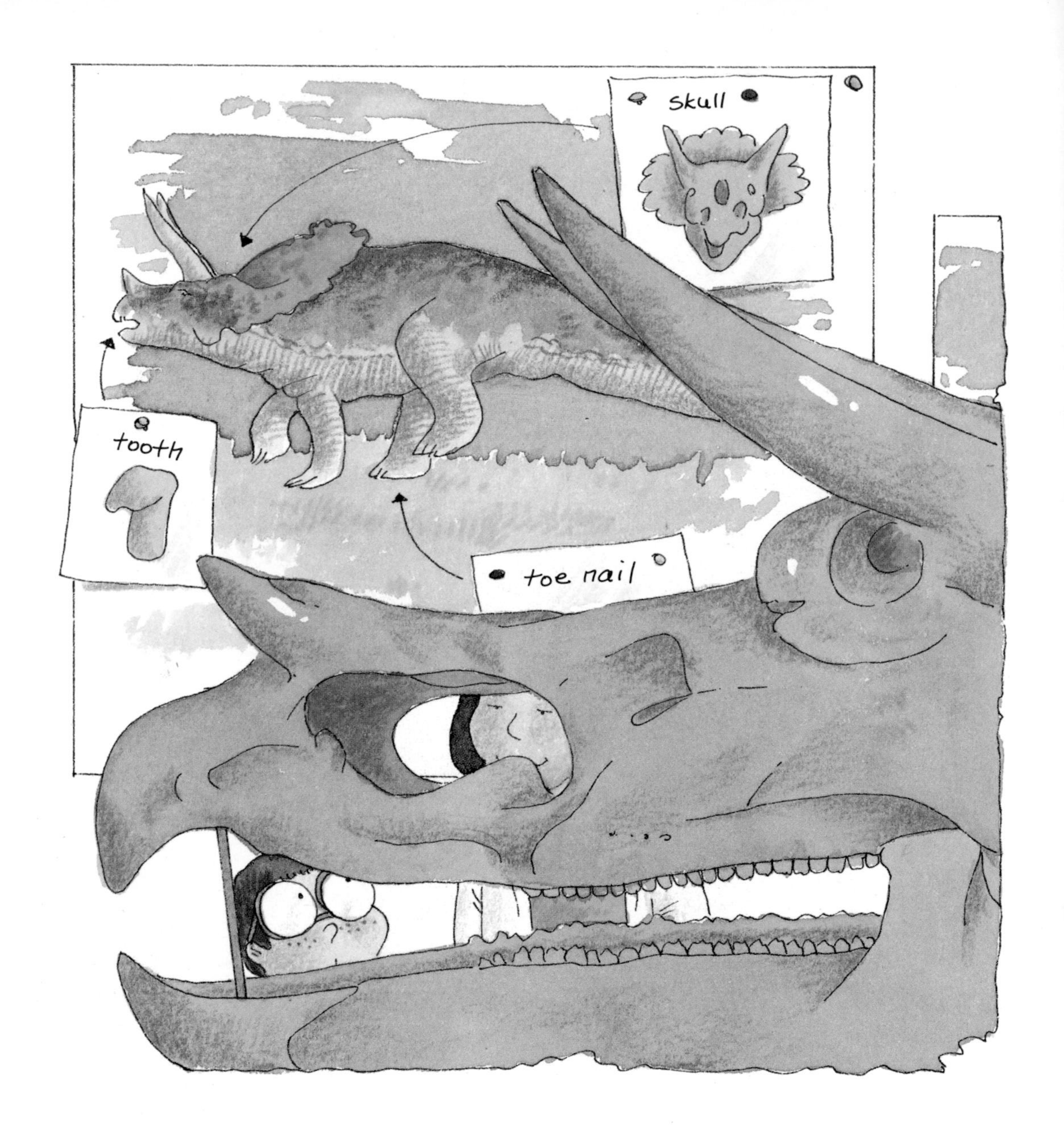

Many of the herbivores were huge, but some were a bit smaller and ate plants closer to the ground. This *Triceratops* had powerful jaws and sharp teeth.

Some dinosaurs were *omnivores*. This means they could eat meat and plants. This *Massospondylus* had many small teeth shaped for chewing any kind of food.

By studying the shape of a dinosaur's leg and backbone, Denise can tell if it walked on two feet or four, and if it moved fast or slowly.

This *Hypsilophodon* had long skinny legs and could probably run 30 miles (48 kilometers) an hour. So, as you can see, not all dinosaurs were big and scary. There were many different kinds.

But now all of them are gone. Where did they go? Well, most scientists agree that dinosaurs, along with lots of other plants and animals, completely disappeared from Earth about 65 million years ago. But no one really knows why.

“Some scientists think that great mountains rose up and changed Earth’s climate. Plant-eating dinosaurs could not eat the new plants that were starting to grow and starved. As they died, so did the meat-eating dinosaurs that ate them.”

"In some places Earth's climate became too cold for the dinosaurs to live. In other places it may have been too dry."

“Some scientists believe that about this time a giant asteroid hit Earth so hard that the explosion sent billions of tons of dust into the atmosphere.”

"Because no light or heat from the sun could get through this dust, the temperature dropped below freezing. Plants died and many dinosaurs had no food. Other dinosaurs were killed by the cold."

"Smaller mammals and birds could find shelter and were protected from the cold by fur and feathers. They ate seeds and roots to stay alive until the dust cleared."

There are many ideas as to why the dinosaurs disappeared. Most scientists now believe that it was several causes, not just one, that wiped them from the face of the Earth.

Today there are no more living dinosaurs, just fossils. But many scientists think that certain descendants of the dinosaurs are still very much alive.

These scientists think that our birds have descended from small meat-eating dinosaurs.

Why do they say this? Aren't dinosaurs more closely related to modern reptiles like lizards or alligators?

Well, take a look at this model of *Archaeopteryx*—a reptile-like bird of the dinosaur period.

Archaeopteryx

Modern Anhinga

It is true that the other dinosaurs had scaly skin and laid eggs like modern reptiles. But, as we have seen, dinosaurs' bones, especially the bones of their legs and hips, were very different.

And since birds, which also lay eggs, have legs that are very similar to those of dinosaurs, scientists now think these two types of animals are closely related.

We know a lot about the dinosaurs, but there is still a lot to learn.

Every time we find a fossil—even just a bone, egg, tooth, or footprint—we can find out more about dinosaurs and why they all died.

Find a small, hard object such as a shell or a plastic toy and completely cover it with a light coat of vegetable oil or petroleum jelly.

Pour a cupful of plaster of paris into a bowl, add a little water, and stir. Add more water until the mixture is like heavy cream. This will be the soft "mud" in which your "fossil" will be formed.

Pour the mixture onto a paper plate.

Wait a few minutes until the plaster begins to get thick. Then, put your shell or other object into it. Push it in only up to its widest part.

When the plaster is almost dry, carefully lift the object out. There, left in the plaster, is the shape—or imprint—of your "fossil." Let the imprint dry overnight. Then you can use it to make a copy of your original object.

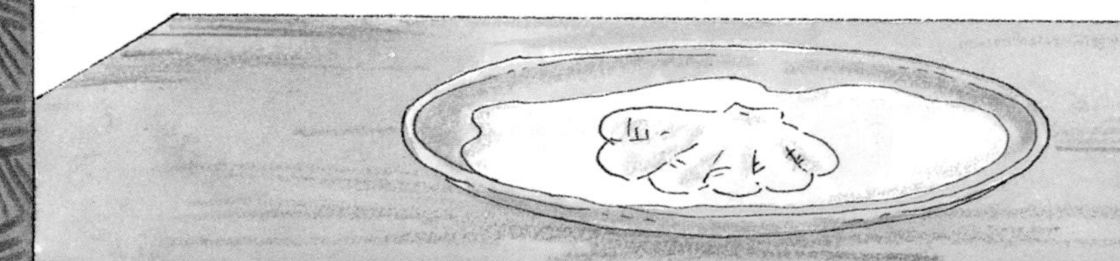

Rub a thin coat of oil or petroleum jelly over the whole surface and the hollow space in the dry plaster.
Mix another cupful of plaster, pour it into your oiled plaster, and let it dry for an hour or more.
Then lift it out carefully. Now you have a cast of your fossil imprint.
We certainly have learned more about the animals that lived on Earth millions of years ago before there were any people at all! Bye for now.

Glossary

asteroid A small object like a planet that orbits or travels in outer space between Mars and Jupiter. Asteroids sometimes enter Earth's atmosphere as shooting stars and occasionally fall to the ground.

atmosphere The mixture of gases that surrounds Earth.

bird A warm-blooded animal that lays eggs and has a backbone, feathers, and wings. Some birds, like the ostrich, don't fly.

carnivore A meat-eating animal.

climate The kind of weather found in an area over a long period of time. For example, the climate of Arizona is mostly hot and dry.

descendant An animal or plant that can be traced back to a previous animal or plant. A child is the descendant of its parents, grandparents, great grandparents, and so on.

dinosaur An extinct animal that lived in the Mesozoic period.

fossil The remains, preserved in stone, of an animal or plant that has been dead for many years.

herbivore A vegetable-eating animal.

lizard A reptile that has a long body with scales. Reptiles usually have four legs and a tail that grows to a point.

Mesozoic The period of time in which the dinosaurs lived. It started about 250 million years ago.

mammal A warm-blooded animal that feeds its young with milk. Mammals have hair and a backbone. Humans are mammals.

omnivore An animal that eats both meat and vegetables.

paleontologist A scientist who studies fossils.

reptile A cold-blooded animal that has a backbone, lays eggs, and has a covering of scales or horny plates.

Barron's Educational Series, Inc.
250 Wireless Boulevard
Hauppauge, New York 11788

International Standard Book No. 0-8120-1573-8

Library of Congress Catalog Card No.

PRINTED IN HONG KONG

4567 9927 987654321

Library of Congress Cataloging-in-Publication Data

Cast, C. Vance.
Where did the dinosaurs go? / C. Vance Cast ; illustrated by Sue Wilkinson.
p. cm.
ISBN 0-8120-1573-8
1. Dinosaurs–Juvenile literature. [1.Dinosaurs.]
I. Wilkinson, Sue (Susan), ill. II. Title.
QE862.D5C34 1994
567.9'1–dc20 93-37184
CIP
AC